Live Lent

LIVE AND LEARN ABOUT LENT

Discipleship Ministry Team
Ministry Council
Cumberland Presbyterian Church

January 2013

8207 Traditional Place
Cordova (Memphis), Tennessee 38016

Prepared and published by the Discipleship Ministry Team of the Ministry Council of the Cumberland Presbyterian Church. Written by Jodi Hearn Rush unless otherwise specified. OUO statement by Elinor Swindle Brown.

Funded, in part, by your contributions to Our United Outreach.

First Edition, First Printing, January 2013

ISBN-13: 978-0615743493
ISBN-10: 0615743498

OUR UNITED OUTREACH
Made Possible In Part By Your Tithe To Our United Outreach

Live Lent

LIVE AND LEARN ABOUT LENT

What is Lent?

- Lent is the season of the church year that begins on Ash Wednesday.

- Lent is the 40 days—not including Sundays which are considered "little Easters"—from Ash Wednesday to Easter Sunday.

- Lent is a time to think and reflect about the life, death, and resurrection of Jesus, and the observance of these events in the life of the church.

- Lent can be time for self-examination, reflection, and renewal.

- Traditionally, the season of Lent is known for the act of giving something up—or fasting—from something that is not good for you or that takes your focus away from God, such as too much television time or a favorite food or beverage.

- Many choose to take something on, or add a new practice to their daily life, that is focused on helping others or more focused on God.

- The traditional practices of Lent—prayer, fasting, almsgiving, Bible reading, forgiveness, somber worship styles—are not meant to punish, but to help us grow closer to God by refocusing our time on spiritual practices.

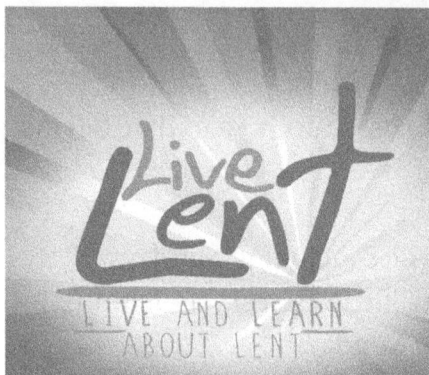

What is Live Lent?

- An invitation for all ages to live and learn about the season of Lent.

- You are invited to join with others from your congregation in focusing on **one Lenten practice a week,** as described in **Live Lent.** In a way, you are trying on these practices to see how they fit. Not all of the practices will be perfect for everyone - but everyone can try them on for size for seven days.

- If you traditionally participate in a Lenten practice, feel free to continue that practice and use **Live Lent** as a devotional book during the Lenten season.

- Special thanks to Dwight Liles, author of **Each Moment Lent To Me**, the poem written especially for **Live Lent**, located on the next page.

How to Use *Live Lent*

- *Live Lent* can be used by individuals to guide your personal Lenten discipline, or can be provided to congregations for a church wide Lenten experience. It is suggested that each family have at least one copy of *Live Lent* for home use.

- As described in *Live Lent*, participants will commit to one practice each week during Lent. A new practice will begin each Sunday during Lent.

- Lent begins on Ash Wednesday; *Live Lent* can be given to church members on Ash Wednesday and the Week One Focus can begin that day or on the first Sunday of Lent.

Additional *Live Lent* Suggestions

- Create a *Live Lent* focus center in your church or at home, each week adding an item that symbolizes the weekly focus. (Example: a Bible for Bible Reading focus, praying hands for Prayer focus, etc.)

- Visit the *Live Lent Facebook* page to see how others are living Lent and to share how you and your family are living Lent.

EACH MOMENT LENT TO ME

This is the fast I have chosen,

to deny the boundary that separates me

from experiencing this universe;

to fully open my eyes and my ears,

to smell and to taste and to feel

what is written in the pages:

the Word that too often I hide from,

When You would hide it in my heart,

take me by Your hand,

teach me how to serve;

that to serve is to reign

in the dream world You imagine,

the world You call Your kingdom,

for which I pray so often without thinking,

without grasping, without weeping

that the real world has so far to go,

before it falls at Your feet in true praise:

not in mere song, but in holy trembling,

that we have walked so arrogantly,

so violently, so selfishly,

So—so forgive me, O God,

that I know not what I do,

that I do not what I know,

that I may know, and do, only Your pleasure

in each moment lent to me.

By Dwight Liles, 12/4/12

LIVE AND LEARN ABOUT LENT

WEEK 1 — Make a Lenten Promise

WEEK 2 — Bible Reading

WEEK 3 — Service

WEEK 4 — Prayer

WEEK 5 — Worship

WEEK 6 — Forgiveness

Week One

Lent is a good time to put God first.

One of the traditional practices of Lent is fasting—
sometimes referred to as *"giving something up for
Lent."* Fasting is the act of removing a food or an
activity from your daily routine. In doing this, you
have more time to focus your attention on God. If
you choose to do a fast, the focus should not be
on what you are giving up, but on God.

Another variation of a fast is to *"take something on,"*
or add an activity to your daily routine that helps
you to focus on God. If you choose to take
something on, this too, is a way to focus more on
God and less on yourself.

Read about fasting in the Bible:

Moses - Exodus 34: 27 - 28
Elijah - I Kings 19: 4 - 16
Fasting & Compassion - Isaiah 58: 6 - 8
Jesus - Matthew 4: I - II
Anna - Luke 2: 36 - 38
Fasting Instructions - Matthew 6: 16 - 18
Before Decisions - Acts 13: I -3; Acts 14: 23

This week—for seven days—you will:

Make a Lenten promise to give up or add an activity to your daily routine that will help you focus more on God and less on yourself.

Promise or Fasting Suggestions

Give up—take a break from it for seven days...

- Television
- Video Games
- Gossiping
- Chocolate or Candy
- Internet
- Complaining
- Soft Drinks
- Eating Out
- Pinterest

Add to your daily schedule for seven days...

- Bible Reading
- A Daily Act of Kindness
- Prayer
- Send cards to people in need
- Community Service
- Quiet Time

Bible Reading

Week Two

Lent is a good time to read your Bible.

Knowing the stories of your faith is an important part of faith formation for all ages.

Read about the importance of reading scripture:

Psalm 119: 105: Your word is a lamp to my feet and a light to my path.

Matthew 28: 19 - 20: Go therefore and make disciples of all nations, baptizing them in the name of the Father and of the Son and of the Holy Spirit, and teaching them to obey everything that I have commanded you. And remember, I am with you always, to the end of the age.

Romans 15:4: For whatever was written in former days was written for our instruction, so that by steadfastness and by the encouragement of the scriptures we might have hope.

This week—for seven days—you will:

Read your Bible each day. Read as many verses as you have time to read, using a version of the Bible or a Bible storybook that is easy to read and understand.

Live Lent uses the New Revised Standard Version of the Bible. For families with children, you might enjoy reading stories from **The Family Story Bible** by Ralph Milton.

<u>Bible Reading Suggestions</u>

Sunday	Mark 1: 9-11	Jesus' Baptism
Monday	Matthew 4: 18-22	Jesus Calls the Disciples
Tuesday	Luke 10: 29-37	Jesus Teaches
Wednesday	Luke 9: 10-17	Jesus' Miracles
Thursday	Luke 22: 39-46	Jesus Prays
Friday	Mark 11: 7-10	Jesus Enters Jerusalem
Saturday	Mark 14: 22-24	Jesus' Last Supper

Service

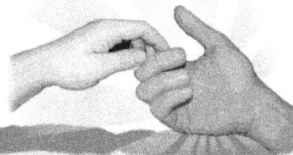

Week Three

Lent is a good time to serve others.

In the Bible there are many examples of people serving others. These stories are examples of how we are to give of our time, talents, and resources to others. The traditional term used during Lent to refer to service is ***almsgiving***—which simply means giving voluntarily to people in need or putting others first.

Read about the importance of serving others:

Deuteronomy 15:11: Since there will never cease to be some in need on the earth, I therefore command you, "Open your hand to the poor and needy neighbor in your land."

Luke 3: 10 - 11: And the crowds asked him, "What then should we do?" In reply he said to them, "Whoever has two coats must share with anyone who has none; and whoever has food must do likewise."

Mark 12:31: You shall love your neighbor as yourself. There is no other commandment greater than these.

This week—for seven days—you will:

Perform acts of service each day.

Service Suggestions

◆ Donate food to a food drive or pantry.

◆ Walk the neighbor's dog.

◆ Give up your place in line and let someone go ahead of you.

◆ Collect your pocket change and give to an organization who feeds people who are hungry.

◆ Give away outgrown clothing or toys.

◆ Assist a neighbor with yard work.

◆ Welcome a new student at school.

◆ Send a card to someone who is sick or unable to leave their home.

◆ Volunteer at church, school, or community organization.

◆ Send a card to someone who is hurting.

Prayer

Week Four

Lent is a good time to pray.

Prayer is the way we communicate or talk with God. This week you are invited to pray each day, using a different form of prayer each day. Some examples are described in the **Prayer Suggestions** on the next page.

Read about times when Jesus prayed:

Luke 6:12: Now during those days he went out to the mountain to pray; and he spent the night in prayer to God.

Luke 11: 1 - 4: He was praying in a certain place, and after he had finished, one of his disciples said to him, "Lord, teach us to pray, as John taught his disciples." He said to them, "When you pray, say: Father, hallowed be your name. Your kingdom come. Give us each day our daily bread. And forgive us our sins, for we ourselves forgive everyone indebted to us. And do not bring us to the time of trial."

Matthew 6:6: But whenever you pray, go into your room and shut the door and pray to your Father who is in secret; and your Father who sees in secret will reward you.

This week—for seven days—you will:

Pray each day.

Prayer Suggestions

- **Pray for a different group each day.**

Sunday	World & Community Leaders
Monday	Your Denomination & Leaders
Tuesday	Friends & Neighbors
Wednesday	Your Local Church
Thursday	Family Members
Friday	Someone You Do Not Know
Saturday	Personal Needs or Concerns

- **If you are not in the habit of praying before meals, give it a try this week.**

- **Newspaper Prayer**
  Read the daily headlines and say the following prayer sentence after each:

  Lord in your mercy, hear my prayer.

- **Open-Ended Prayer**
  Complete the following statements as your prayer:
  God, you are...
  I thank you for...
  Forgive me for....
  Give me strength for...
  As I talk to you I feel...

Worship

Week Five

Lent is a good time to worship.

But, in a different way! Worship styles during Lent are different from other times of the church year, possibly more somber and lacking the praise language that you are accustomed to at other times of the year. If you have noticed this - good! It is intentionally planned this way to match the Lenten season of reflection and to be in contrast with the joyous celebration that comes on Easter.

Read scriptures about worship:

John 4:24: God is spirit, and those who worship him must worship in spirit and truth.

Luke 4:8: Jesus answered him, "It is written, 'Worship the Lord your God, and serve only him.'"

Psalm 95:6: O come, let us worship and bow down, let us kneel before the Lord, our Maker!

Psalm 46:10: Be still, and know that I am God.

This week—for seven days—you will:

Notice how the season of Lent is reflected in your worship service.

Lenten Worship Suggestions

♦ A custom in some churches is to "say goodbye to the alleluias" during Lent. By not speaking or singing the word "Alleluia" during the season, there is a greater appreciation and meaning to the word on its return on Easter Sunday.

♦ Flowers and decorative items may be removed from the sanctuary to encourage the mood of penitence and reflection during Lent. This contributes to the joy and beauty of Easter Sunday when these decorations return.

♦ The words of the worship hymns and liturgy during the season of Lent are rich with imagery that remind us of Christ's sacrifice. Notice the words in the worship service that directly reflect the season of Lent.

♦ Sing or read the words of these Lenten hymns:
When I Survey the Wondrous Cross
Abide With Me
O Sacred Head, Now Wounded

Week Six

Lent is a good time to say, "I'm sorry" and "I am forgiven."

As Lent is coming to an end, we recall that Jesus' death happened because of our sin. This week and every week we can give and receive forgiveness for our sins and celebrate the wonderful truth that in Jesus Christ we are forgiven!

Read scriptures about forgiveness:

1 John 1: 9: If we confess our sins, he who is faithful and just will forgive us our sins and cleanse us from all unrighteousness.

Acts 3: 19: Repent therefore, and turn to God so that your sins may be wiped out.

Matthew 6: 14: For if you forgive others their trespasses, your heavenly Father will also forgive you.

Matthew 26: 27 - 28: Then he took a cup, and after giving thanks he gave it to them, saying, "Drink from it, all of you; for this is my blood of the covenant, which is poured out for many for the forgiveness of sins."

This week—for seven days—you will:

Forgive others and receive forgiveness.

Steps to Forgiveness

♦ Think about a choice you have made that hurt someone.

♦ Think about someone that has hurt you.

♦ Tell God about these things by writing them down, drawing a picture, or simple talking to God through prayer.

♦ Know that if you ask God for forgiveness—you are forgiven!

♦ Find a time to tell the person you hurt, that you are sorry.

What is *Our United Outreach*?

Our United Outreach is a vital part of funding for the Cumberland Presbyterian Church as it comes together as a covenant community to fulfill its vision of ministry. As recorded in the 1985 General Assembly minutes regarding Our United Outreach, Cumberland Presbyterians have voluntarily given ten percent of their church's income to help others grow in their mission, education and stewardship.

We have always been a people of diversity. At times, we have embraced this and at times we have rejected it. Our vision is that this can be a point of celebration illustrated beautifully through our unified giving to one purpose: to fulfill God's will on earth.

Together through the giving of Our United Outreach funds, Cumberland Presbyterians are reaching out to those in need. We have heard the cries of those in need and have been willing to give of our abundance to those without such an abundance. Through Our United Outreach, our ministries can overflow into the lives of others giving comfort where there is pain, healing where there is hurt.

Our United Outreach is the grateful response to God in an orderly and responsible manner. It is not intended to be a burden, but a way to express our gratitude to God for what God has done for us. It is an avenue to share God's good news with the global community. When a Christian shares his/her gifts with the church, those gifts, whether small or large, are shared with the whole church because the church is one.

As God continues to give the Cumberland Presbyterian Church a clearer vision to move forward with our ministry, may God also give us ever grateful hearts to see the need and together work toward being the presence of Jesus Christ in the world.

Cumberland Presbyterian Resources

Curriculum, Books, Church Supplies

by, for, and about Cumberland Presbyterians and the Reformed Tradition!

www.ingramcontent.com/pod-product-compliance
Lightning Source LLC
Chambersburg PA
CBHW031337040426
42443CB00005B/374